Slow Cooker

Slow Cooker

Over 70 fuss-free ideas for simple everyday dishes

This edition published in 2011
LOVE FOOD is an imprint of Parragon Books Ltd

Parragon
Queen Street House
4 Queen Street
Bath BA1 1HE, UK

ISBN: 978-1-4454-2017-2

Printed in China

Cover photography by Mike Cooper
Additional photography by Clive Streeter
Additional home economy by Teresa Goldfinch
Introduction and additional recipes by Linda Doeser

NOTES FOR THE READER
This book uses imperial, metric, and US cup measurements. Follow the same units of measurement
throughout; do not mix imperial and metric. All spoon measurements are level: teaspoons are assumed
to be 5 ml, and tablespoons are assumed to be 15 ml. Unless otherwise stated, milk is assumed to be
whole, eggs and individual vegetables are medium, and pepper is freshly ground black pepper.

The times given are an approximate guide only. Preparation times differ according to the techniques
used by different people and the cooking times may also vary from those given. Optional ingredients,
variations, or serving suggestions have not been included in the calculations.

Recipes using raw or very lightly cooked eggs should be avoided by infants, the elderly, pregnant
women, convalescents, and anyone with a chronic condition. Pregnant and breast-feeding women are
advised to avoid eating peanuts and peanut products. People with a nut allergy should be aware that
some of the prepared ingredients used in the recipes in this book may contain nuts. Always check the
package before use.

Contents

Introduction

Using a slow cooker is an easy, time-saving, versatile, and economical way to cook healthy and delicious meals. It's the perfect choice, whatever your lifestyle, whether you're a cash-strapped student, a young couple with demanding careers and a hectic social life, a busy family with young children and a tight budget, or retirees wanting to make the most of your rediscovered leisure time.

Slow cooking is easy, even for amateur cooks, because everything goes into one pot after less than half an hour's preparation and it can then be safely left to cook for anywhere up to 10 hours while you get on with your life. Less of your valuable time is spent standing at the stove watching over pots and pans, and cleaning up afterward is quick, too, because there is often only one pot to wash. The slow cooker is a versatile piece of kitchen equipment because it can be used for so many different kinds of dishes—not just substantial casseroles and stews, but soups, fish dishes, pot roasts, risottos, steamed sponge cakes, and delicious desserts. Because the amount of electricity needed to power a slow cooker is very low, it is much more economical than baking a single dish in the oven. In addition, because the food cooks slowly, it is perfect for tenderizing less expensive but tougher cuts of meat. As food cooks in a slow cooker, steam condenses on the inside of the lid, forming a seal, which not only keeps the ingredients moist but also locks in the nutrients and flavor.

Using a slow cooker

When buying a slow cooker, bear in mind the size of your family and available storage space. A standard 4-quart slow cooker is perfect for the average family, but a smaller model would suit a single person and a larger one a big family or someone who entertains frequently.

Models vary from one manufacturer to another, so it is essential to read the instructions supplied with your particular cooker. That said, the basics apply to all models.

Always stand the cooker on a level counter and keep the cord out of reach of small children and pets. Before plugging it in, make sure the control is switched to the off position. Older models may require preheating before the ingredients are added, but this is not usually necessary for modern slow cookers—check the manufacturer's instructions. Note that preheating an empty cooker that does not require it will cause damage.

Remove the cooking pot from the base unit before adding the ingredients. This prevents spills inside the base unit, which are difficult to clean and may damage the slow cooker. Similarly, remove the pot from the base unit before serving—and make sure that you use oven mitts because it will be hot.

For maximum efficiency, the cooking pot should always be at least half full and may be filled to two-thirds. There should always be 2 inches/5 cm between the level of the food and the top of the cooker. A single cut of meat should occupy no more than two-thirds of the cooking pot. When using the slow cooker for steaming, put a trivet in the bottom. An upturned small plate works well in a round cooker and an upturned cookie cutter in an oval one. Make sure there is a gap of 3/4 inch/ 2 cm all around a heatproof bowl in a round cooker and a gap of 1/2 inch/1 cm between the bowl and the narrowest part of the cooking pot in an oval cooker.

When preparing savory dishes, meat is usually browned first and vegetables, such as onions and carrots, are softened in a pan or skillet on the stove. Liquid, such as stock, is then added and brought to a boil before the mixture is transferred to the slow cooker. Cold, but not frozen, ingredients may be put directly into the slow cooker, but the liquid should always be heated before it is added. If using frozen ingredients, let them thaw thoroughly before adding to the cooker. Do not use the slow cooker for reheating leftovers—transfer to a pan or casserole and reheat on the stove or in the oven.

Once the ingredients have been added to the cooker and it has been covered with the lid and switched on, resist the temptation to uncover and stir during the first half of the cooking time. This breaks the water seal and reduces the temperature. If the recipe recommends stirring or adding extra ingredients part of the way through the second half of the cooking

time, do this as quickly as possible. Otherwise, leave the dish alone.

When you are ready to serve, turn the control to the off position and switch off the power. Lift out the cooking pot, using oven mitts, and put it on a mat or trivet as it will be hot. Do not lean over the pot when removing the lid because the steam might scald you.

Wash the cooking pot in hot soapy water. If any food has stuck during cooking, let the pot soak. Do not use scourers or abrasive cleaners. Never immerse the base unit in water—simply wipe off any splashes with a damp cloth. If you have an older model with an integrated cooking pot that cannot be removed, do not immerse it in water.

Everyday

Traditional Beef Stew

serves 6

4 tbsp all-purpose flour

2 lb 4 oz/1 kg braising beef,
cut into 1½-inch/4-cm
cubes

2 tbsp sunflower oil

3 slices bacon, chopped

4 tbsp butter

2 onions, thinly sliced

4 carrots, sliced

1 lb 5 oz/600 g potatoes,
cut into chunks

1⅔ cups sliced mushrooms

1 bay leaf

2 fresh thyme sprigs,
finely chopped, plus
extra sprigs to garnish

1 tbsp finely chopped fresh
parsley

14 oz/400 g canned
chopped tomatoes

1½ cups beef stock

salt and pepper

Put the flour into a plastic food bag and season well with salt and pepper. Add the beef cubes, in batches, hold the top securely, and shake well to coat. Transfer the meat to a plate.

Heat the oil in a large skillet. Add the bacon and cook over low heat, stirring frequently, for 5 minutes. Add the beef cubes, increase the heat to medium, and cook, stirring frequently, for 8–10 minutes, until evenly browned. Remove the meat with a slotted spoon and set aside on a plate.

Wipe out the skillet with paper towels, then return to low heat and melt the butter. Add the onions and cook, stirring occasionally, for 5 minutes, until softened. Add the carrots, potatoes, and mushrooms and cook, stirring occasionally, for an additional 5 minutes.

Season to taste with salt and pepper, add the bay leaf, chopped thyme, parsley, and tomatoes, and pour in the stock. Bring to a boil, stirring occasionally, then remove the skillet from the heat, and transfer the mixture to the slow cooker. Stir in the meat, cover, and cook on low for 8–9 hours.

Remove and discard the bay leaf. Garnish with thyme sprigs and serve immediately.

Tagliatelle with Meat Sauce

serves 6

3 tbsp olive oil

3 slices bacon, chopped

1 onion, chopped

1 garlic clove, finely chopped

1 carrot, chopped

1 celery stalk, chopped

1 lb/450 g ground beef

½ cup red wine

2 tbsp tomato paste

14 oz/400 g canned chopped tomatoes

1¼ cups beef stock

½ tsp dried oregano

1 bay leaf

1 lb/450 g dried tagliatelle

salt and pepper

grated Parmesan cheese, to serve

Heat the oil in a pan. Add the bacon and cook over medium heat, stirring frequently, for 3 minutes. Reduce the heat, add the onion, garlic, carrot, and celery and cook, stirring occasionally, for 5 minutes, until the vegetables have softened.

Increase the heat to medium and add the ground beef. Cook, stirring frequently and breaking it up with a wooden spoon, for 8–10 minutes, until evenly browned. Pour in the wine and cook for a few minutes, until the alcohol has evaporated, then stir in the tomato paste, tomatoes, stock, oregano, and bay leaf and season to taste with salt and pepper.

Bring to a boil, then transfer to the slow cooker. Cover and cook on low for 8–8½ hours.

Shortly before serving, bring a large pan of lightly salted water to a boil. Add the pasta, bring back to a boil, and cook for 8–10 minutes, until tender but still firm to the bite. Drain and put into a warmed serving bowl. Remove and discard the bay leaf, then add the meat sauce to the pasta. Toss with 2 forks, sprinkle with the Parmesan, and serve immediately.

Lamb & Rice Soup

serves 6

2 lb 4 oz/1 kg boned leg of
lamb, cut into
1-inch/2.5-cm cubes

2 lamb bones, cracked

3 garlic cloves, peeled

8¾ cups water

scant ½ cup long-grain rice

6 slices French bread

2 tbsp chopped fresh
parsley

salt and pepper

Put the lamb, lamb bones, and garlic cloves into a large pan and pour in the water. Season well with salt and pepper and bring to a boil, skimming off any foam that rises to the surface. Transfer the mixture to the slow cooker, cover, and cook on low for 5 hours.

Meanwhile, soak the rice in several changes of cold water for 30 minutes, then drain.

Remove and discard the lamb bones and garlic cloves from the slow cooker, then stir in the rice. Re-cover and cook on low for an additional 2–2½ hours, until the lamb and rice are tender.

Shortly before serving, preheat the broiler. Place the bread slices on the broiler rack and lightly broil on both sides. Put 1 piece of bread into each individual serving bowl. Ladle the soup over the bread, sprinkle with the parsley, and serve immediately.

Pork with Apple & Herbs

serves 6

2 tbsp all-purpose flour

1 lb 12 oz/800 g boneless pork, cut into 1-inch/ 2.5-cm cubes

5 tbsp sunflower oil

1 large onion, chopped

2 garlic cloves, finely chopped

2 apples, cored and cut into wedges

1¼ cups hard cider or apple juice

2½ cups chicken stock

2 bay leaves

2 fresh sage sprigs

1 fresh rosemary sprig

3 tbsp chopped fresh parsley

salt and pepper

mashed potatoes, to serve

Put the flour into a plastic food bag and season well with salt and pepper. Add the pork cubes, in batches, hold the top securely, and shake well to coat. Transfer the meat to a plate.

Heat 3 tablespoons of the oil in a large skillet. Add the pork cubes, in batches if necessary, and cook over medium heat, stirring frequently, for 5–8 minutes, until evenly browned. Transfer to a plate and set aside.

Add the remaining oil to the skillet and heat. Add the onion and garlic and cook over low heat, stirring occasionally, for 10 minutes, until softened and lightly browned. Add the apple wedges and cook, stirring occasionally, for 3–5 minutes, until beginning to color. Gradually stir in the hard cider and stock, scraping up any sediment from the bottom of the skillet, and bring to a boil. Season to taste with salt and pepper, add the bay leaves and the sage and rosemary sprigs, and transfer to the slow cooker. Stir in the pork, cover, and cook on low for 6–7 hours.

Remove and discard the bay leaves and the sage and rosemary sprigs. Transfer the stew to warmed individual plates and sprinkle with the parsley. Serve immediately with mashed potatoes.

Boston Baked Beans

serves 4–6

2½ cups dried navy beans, soaked overnight and drained

about 6¼ cups boiling water

4 oz/115 g slab bacon

2 tbsp ketchup

3 tbsp molasses

1½ tbsp dark brown sugar

2 tsp dry mustard

1 onion, chopped

salt and pepper

Place the beans in the slow cooker and add the boiling water, making sure that the beans are covered. Cover and cook on high for 3 hours. Meanwhile, cut the bacon into chunks.

Drain the beans, reserving 1 cup of the cooking liquid. Mix the reserved liquid with the ketchup, molasses, sugar, mustard, and 1 teaspoon of salt.

Return the beans to the slow cooker and add the bacon, onion, and the molasses mixture. Stir, then cover and cook on low for 11 hours.

Taste and adjust the seasoning, adding salt and pepper if needed. Serve immediately.

Sausage & Bean Stew

serves 4

2 tbsp sunflower oil

2 onions, chopped

2 garlic cloves, finely chopped

4 slices bacon, chopped

1 lb 2 oz/500 g pork sausages

14 oz/400 g canned navy beans, red kidney beans, or black-eyed peas, drained and rinsed

2 tbsp chopped fresh parsley

⅔ cup hot beef stock

to serve

4 slices French bread

½ cup grated Swiss cheese

Heat the oil in a heavy skillet. Add the onions and cook over low heat, stirring occasionally, for 5 minutes, until softened. Add the garlic, bacon, and sausages, and cook, stirring and turning the sausages occasionally, for an additional 5 minutes.

Using a slotted spoon, transfer the mixture from the skillet to the slow cooker. Add the beans, parsley, and stock, then cover and cook on low for 6 hours.

Shortly before serving, preheat the broiler. Place the bread slices on the broiler rack and lightly broil on 1 side under the preheated broiler. Divide the grated cheese among the untoasted sides of the bread slices and place under the broiler until just melted.

Ladle the stew onto warmed plates, top each portion with a slice of cheese-topped toast, and serve immediately.

Chicken Stew

serves 4

3 tbsp corn oil

1 large onion, thinly sliced

1 green bell pepper, seeded and chopped

8 chicken portions, such as thighs and drumsticks

14 oz/400 g canned chopped tomatoes, drained

pinch of cayenne pepper

1 tbsp Worcestershire sauce

1¼ cups hot chicken stock

1 tbsp cornstarch

2–3 tbsp water

generous 1 cup frozen corn kernels, thawed

generous 3 cups frozen fava beans, thawed

salt

Heat the oil in a large heavy skillet. Add the onion and bell pepper and cook over medium heat, stirring occasionally, for 5 minutes, until the onion is softened. Using a slotted spoon, transfer the mixture to the slow cooker.

Add the chicken to the skillet and cook, turning occasionally, for 5 minutes, until golden all over. Transfer to the slow cooker and add the tomatoes. Season with the cayenne pepper and salt to taste. Stir the Worcestershire sauce into the hot stock and pour into the slow cooker. Cover and cook on low for 6½ hours.

Mix the cornstarch to a paste with the water and stir into the stew. Add the corn and fava beans, re-cover, and cook on high for 30–40 minutes, until the chicken is tender and cooked through. Transfer to warmed plates and serve immediately.

Easy Chinese Chicken

serves 4

2 tsp grated fresh ginger

4 garlic cloves, finely chopped

2 star anise

⅔ cup Chinese rice wine or medium dry sherry

2 tbsp dark soy sauce

1 tsp sesame oil

5 tbsp water

4 skinless chicken thighs or drumsticks

shredded scallions, to garnish

cooked rice, to serve

Combine the ginger, garlic, star anise, rice wine, soy sauce, sesame oil, and water in a bowl. Place the chicken in a pan, add the spice mixture, and bring to a boil.

Transfer to the slow cooker, cover, and cook on low for 4 hours, or until the chicken is tender and cooked through.

Remove and discard the star anise. Transfer the chicken to warmed plates, garnish with shredded scallions, and serve immediately with rice.

Chicken & Apple Stew

serves 4

1 tbsp olive oil

4 chicken portions, about 6 oz/175 g each

1 onion, chopped

2 celery stalks, coarsely chopped

1½ tbsp all-purpose flour

1¼ cups apple juice

⅔ cup chicken stock

1 baking apple, cored and cut into quarters

2 bay leaves

1–2 tsp honey

1 yellow bell pepper, seeded and cut into chunks

salt and pepper

to garnish

1 large or 2 medium apples, cored and sliced

1 tbsp melted butter

2 tbsp raw brown sugar

1 tbsp chopped fresh mint

Heat the oil in a heavy skillet. Add the chicken and cook over medium–high heat, turning frequently, for 10 minutes, until golden brown all over. Using a slotted spoon, transfer the chicken to the slow cooker.

Add the onion and celery to the skillet and cook over low heat, stirring occasionally, for 5 minutes, until softened. Sprinkle in the flour and cook, stirring constantly, for 2 minutes, then remove the skillet from the heat. Gradually stir in the apple juice and stock, then return the skillet to the heat and bring to a boil, stirring constantly. Stir in the baking apple, bay leaves, and honey and season to taste with salt and pepper.

Pour the mixture over the chicken in the slow cooker, cover, and cook on low for 6½ hours, until the chicken is tender and cooked through. Stir in the bell pepper, re-cover, and cook on high for 45 minutes.

Shortly before serving, preheat the broiler. Brush one side of the apple slices with half the melted butter and sprinkle with half the sugar. Cook under the preheated broiler for 2–3 minutes, until the sugar has caramelized. Turn the slices over with tongs, brush with the remaining butter, and sprinkle with the remaining sugar. Broil for an additional 2 minutes.

Remove and discard the bay leaves, then transfer the stew to warmed plates and garnish with the caramelized apple slices and the mint. Serve immediately.

Sea Bass in Lemon Sauce

serves 4

8 sea bass fillets

4 tbsp unsalted butter

4 tbsp all-purpose flour

3¾ cups warm milk

4 tbsp lemon juice

3¼ cups sliced mushrooms

1 bouquet garni

salt and pepper

lemon wedges and grilled asparagus, to serve

Put the fish fillets into the slow cooker and set aside.

Melt the butter in a pan over low heat. Add the flour and cook, stirring constantly, for 1 minute. Gradually stir in the milk, a little at a time, and bring to a boil, stirring constantly. Stir in the lemon juice and mushrooms, add the bouquet garni, and season to taste with salt and pepper. Reduce the heat and simmer for 5 minutes. Pour the sauce over the fish fillets, cover, and cook on low for 1½ hours.

Carefully lift out the fish fillets and put them on warmed individual plates. Remove and discard the bouquet garni and spoon the sauce over the fish. Serve immediately with lemon wedges and asparagus.

Tilapia with Fennel & Orange Juice

serves 4

4 whole tilapia, about
12 oz/350 g each, cleaned

1 orange, halved and
thinly sliced

2 garlic cloves, thinly sliced

6 fresh thyme sprigs

1 tbsp olive oil

1 fennel bulb, thinly sliced

2 cups orange juice

1 bay leaf

1 tsp dill seeds

salt and pepper

salad greens, to serve

Season the fish inside and outside with salt and pepper. Make 3–4 diagonal slashes on each side. Divide the orange slices among the cavities and add 2–3 garlic slices and a thyme sprig to each. Chop the remaining thyme sprigs and put in the slashes with the remaining garlic slices.

Heat the oil in a large skillet. Add the fennel and cook over medium heat, stirring frequently, for 3–5 minutes, until just softened. Add the orange juice and bay leaf and bring to a boil, then reduce the heat and simmer for 5 minutes.

Transfer the fennel mixture to the slow cooker. Put the fish on top and sprinkle with the dill seeds. Cover and cook on high for 1¼–1½ hours, until the flesh flakes easily.

Carefully transfer the fish to 4 warmed plates. Remove and discard the bay leaf and spoon the fennel and some of the cooking juices over the fish. Serve immediately with salad greens.

Summer Vegetable Casserole

serves 4

14 oz/400 g canned cannellini beans, drained and rinsed

14 oz/400 g canned artichoke hearts, drained

1 red bell pepper, seeded and sliced

4 small turnips, sliced

2⅔ cups baby spinach leaves, coarse stalks removed

6 thyme sprigs

14 oz/400 g frozen baby fava beans

1 tbsp olive oil

2 tbsp butter

4 shallots, chopped

4 leeks, sliced

3 celery stalks, sliced

3 tbsp all-purpose flour

scant 1 cup dry white wine

⅔ cup vegetable stock

salt and pepper

Put the cannellini beans, artichoke hearts, bell pepper, turnips, spinach, and 4 of the thyme sprigs into the slow cooker.

Cook the fava beans in a small pan of lightly salted boiling water for 10 minutes.

Meanwhile, heat the oil and butter in a large skillet. Add the shallots, leeks, and celery and cook over low heat, stirring occasionally, for 5 minutes, until softened. Stir in the flour and cook, stirring constantly, for 1 minute. Gradually stir in the wine and stock and bring to a boil, stirring constantly. Season to taste with salt and pepper.

Transfer the contents of the skillet to the slow cooker. Drain the fava beans and add to the slow cooker. Stir well, cover, and cook on low for 2½–3 hours. Remove and discard the thyme sprigs. Sprinkle with the leaves from the remaining thyme sprigs and serve immediately.

Tomato & Lentil Soup

serves 4

2 tbsp sunflower oil

1 onion, chopped

1 garlic clove, finely chopped

2 celery stalks, chopped

2 carrots, chopped

1 tsp ground cumin

1 tsp ground coriander

¾ cup red or yellow lentils

1 tbsp tomato paste

5 cups vegetable stock

14 oz/400 g canned chopped tomatoes

1 bay leaf

salt and pepper

sour cream and toasted crusty bread, to serve

Heat the oil in a pan. Add the onion and garlic and cook over low heat, stirring occasionally, for 5 minutes, until softened. Stir in the celery and carrots and cook, stirring occasionally, for an additional 4 minutes. Stir in the cumin and coriander and cook, stirring, for 1 minute, then add the lentils.

Mix the tomato paste with a little of the stock in a small bowl and add to the pan with the remaining stock, the tomatoes, and bay leaf. Bring to a boil, then transfer to the slow cooker. Stir well, cover, and cook on low for 3½–4 hours.

Remove and discard the bay leaf. Transfer the soup to a food processor or blender and process until smooth. Season to taste with salt and pepper. Ladle into warmed soup bowls, top each with a swirl of sour cream, and serve immediately with toasted crusty bread.

Mixed Bean Chili

serves 4–6

2 tbsp corn oil

1 onion, chopped

1 garlic clove, finely chopped

1 fresh red chile, seeded and chopped

1 yellow bell pepper, seeded and chopped

1 tsp ground cumin

1 tbsp chili powder

⅔ cup dried red kidney beans, soaked overnight, drained, and rinsed

⅔ cup dried black beans, soaked overnight, drained, and rinsed

⅔ cup dried pinto beans, soaked overnight, drained, and rinsed

4 cups vegetable stock

1 tbsp sugar

salt and pepper

chopped fresh cilantro, to garnish

crusty bread, to serve

Heat the oil in a large heavy pan. Add the onion, garlic, chile, and bell pepper and cook over medium heat, stirring occasionally, for 5 minutes. Stir in the cumin and chili powder and cook, stirring, for 1–2 minutes. Add the drained beans and stock and bring to a boil. Boil vigorously for 15 minutes.

Transfer the mixture to the slow cooker, cover, and cook on low for 10 hours, until the beans are tender.

Season to taste with salt and pepper, then ladle about one-third into a bowl. Mash well with a potato masher, then return the mashed beans to the slow cooker and stir in the sugar. Garnish with cilantro and serve immediately with crusty bread.

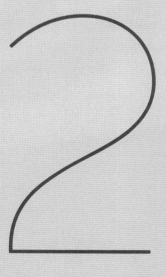

Dinner
Time

Traditional Pot Roast

serves 6

1 onion, finely chopped

4 carrots, sliced

4 small turnips, sliced

4 celery stalks, sliced

2 potatoes, sliced

1 sweet potato, sliced

3–4 lb/1.3–1.8 kg beef
pot roast

1 bouquet garni

1¼ cups hot beef stock

salt and pepper

fresh thyme sprigs,
to garnish

Place the onion, carrots, turnips, celery, potatoes, and sweet potato in the slow cooker and stir to mix well.

Rub the beef all over with salt and pepper, then place on top of the bed of vegetables. Add the bouquet garni and pour in the stock. Cover and cook on low for 9–10 hours, until the beef is cooked to your liking.

Transfer the beef and vegetables to a warmed serving dish. Garnish with thyme sprigs and serve immediately.

Beef in Beer

serves 4–6

4 tbsp sunflower oil

2 lb 4 oz/1 kg beef pot roast

3 lb 5 oz/1.5 kg red onions, thinly sliced

2¼ cups beef stock

1½ tbsp all-purpose flour

1½ cups beer

3 garlic cloves, chopped

1 strip thinly pared lemon rind

1 bay leaf

2 tbsp molasses

salt and pepper

fresh flat-leaf parsley sprigs, to garnish

Heat the oil in a large skillet. Add the beef and cook over medium–high heat, turning occasionally, for 5–8 minutes, until evenly browned. Transfer the beef to the slow cooker.

Reduce the heat to low and add the onions to the skillet. Cook, stirring occasionally, for 5 minutes, until softened. Stir in 2 tablespoons of the stock, scraping up the sediment from the bottom of the skillet, and cook until all the liquid has evaporated. Add another 2 tablespoons of the stock and continue to cook for an additional 15 minutes, adding 2 tablespoons of the stock each time the previous addition has evaporated.

Stir in the flour and cook, stirring constantly, for 1 minute, then gradually stir in the remaining stock and the beer. Increase the heat to medium and bring to a boil, stirring constantly.

Stir in the garlic, lemon rind, bay leaf, and molasses and season to taste with salt and pepper. Transfer the onion mixture to the slow cooker, cover, and cook on low for 8–9 hours, until the beef is cooked to your liking.

Remove the beef, carve into slices, and arrange on a warmed serving dish. Remove and discard the lemon rind and bay leaf. Spoon the cooking juices over the meat, garnish with parsley sprigs, and serve immediately.

Pork & Beans

serves 4

2 tbsp sunflower oil

4 pork chops, trimmed of excess fat

1 onion, chopped

14 oz/400 g canned chopped tomatoes

15 oz/425 g canned baked beans

butter, for greasing, plus extra for browning (optional)

1 lb 9 oz/700 g potatoes, thinly sliced

scant 2 cups hot chicken stock

salt and pepper

Heat the oil in a skillet. Season the chops well with salt and pepper, add to the skillet, and cook over medium heat for 2–3 minutes on each side, until evenly browned. Remove the skillet from the heat and transfer the chops to a plate.

Combine the onion, tomatoes, and baked beans in a bowl and season well with salt and pepper.

Lightly grease the slow cooker pot, then make a layer of half the potatoes in the bottom. Cover with half the tomato-and-bean mixture. Put the chops on top, then add the remaining tomato-and-bean mixture. Cover with the remaining potato slices. Pour in the stock, cover, and cook on low for 8–10 hours.

If desired, dot the topping with butter, then place the slow cooker pot under a preheated broiler to brown the potatoes before serving.

Cured Ham Cooked in Hard Cider

serves 6

2 lb 4 oz/1 kg boneless cured ham in a single piece

1 onion, halved

4 cloves

6 black peppercorns

1 tsp juniper berries

1 celery stalk, chopped

1 carrot, sliced

3 cups hard cider

Place a trivet or rack in the slow cooker, if you like, and stand the ham on it. Otherwise, just place the ham in the cooker. Stud each of the onion halves with 2 of the cloves and add to the slow cooker with the peppercorns, juniper berries, celery, and carrot.

Pour in the hard cider, cover, and cook on low for 8 hours, until the meat is tender.

Remove the ham from the cooker and place on a board. Loosely cover with foil and let stand for 10–15 minutes. Discard the cooking liquid and flavorings.

Cut off any rind and fat from the ham, then carve into slices and serve immediately.

Lamb with Spring Vegetables & Barley

serves 4–6

5 tbsp olive oil

6 shallots, chopped

1 garlic clove, chopped

2 celery stalks, chopped

2 tbsp all-purpose flour

1 lb 9 oz/700 g boned leg or shoulder of lamb, cut into 1-inch/2.5-cm cubes

3¾ cups chicken stock

½ cup pearl barley, rinsed

2–3 small turnips, halved

8–10 baby carrots

2 cups frozen young green peas, thawed

1⅔ cups frozen baby fava beans, thawed

salt and pepper

chopped fresh parsley, to garnish

Heat 3 tablespoons of the oil in a large pan. Add the shallots, garlic, and celery and cook over low heat, stirring occasionally, for 8–10 minutes, until softened and lightly browned.

Meanwhile, put the flour into a plastic food bag and season well with salt and pepper. Add the lamb cubes, in batches, hold the top securely, and shake well to coat. Transfer the meat to a plate.

Using a slotted spoon, transfer the vegetables to the slow cooker. Add the remaining oil to the pan and heat. Add the lamb, in batches if necessary, increase the heat to medium, and cook, stirring frequently, for 8–10 minutes, until evenly browned.

Return all the lamb to the pan. Gradually stir in the stock, scraping up any sediment from the bottom of the pan. Stir in the pearl barley, turnips, and carrots, season to taste with salt and pepper, and bring to a boil. Transfer the mixture to the slow cooker and stir well. Cover and cook on low for 8–10 hours, until the lamb is tender.

Add the peas and fava beans to the slow cooker, sprinkling them evenly on top of the stew. Re-cover and cook on low for an additional 30 minutes, until heated through. Stir well, then taste and adjust the seasoning, adding salt and pepper if needed. Garnish with parsley and serve immediately.

Venison Casserole

serves 6

3 tbsp olive oil

2 lb 4 oz/1 kg braising venison, cut into 1¼-inch/3-cm cubes

2 onions, thinly sliced

2 garlic cloves, chopped

1½ cups beef stock

2 tbsp all-purpose flour

½ cup port

2 tbsp red currant jelly

6 juniper berries, crushed

4 cloves, crushed

pinch of ground cinnamon

pinch of freshly grated nutmeg

salt and pepper

chopped fresh flat-leaf parsley, to garnish

mashed potatoes, to serve

Heat the oil in a heavy skillet. Add the venison and cook over high heat, stirring frequently, for 5 minutes, until evenly browned. Using a slotted spoon, transfer the meat to the slow cooker.

Add the onions and garlic to the skillet, reduce the heat, and cook, stirring occasionally, for 5 minutes, until softened. Transfer them to the slow cooker.

Gradually stir the stock into the skillet, scraping up any sediment from the bottom, then bring to a boil, stirring constantly. Sprinkle the flour over the meat in the slow cooker and stir well to coat evenly. Stir in the hot stock, then add the port, red currant jelly, juniper berries, cloves, cinnamon, and nutmeg. Season to taste with salt and pepper. Cover and cook on low for 7–8 hours, until the meat is tender.

Taste and adjust the seasoning, adding salt and pepper if needed. Remove and discard the cloves. Garnish with parsley and serve immediately with mashed potatoes.

Chicken Braised with Red Cabbage

serves 4

2 tbsp sunflower oil

4 skinless chicken thighs or drumsticks

1 onion, chopped

5½ cups shredded red cabbage

2 apples, peeled and chopped

12 canned or cooked chestnuts, halved (optional)

½ tsp juniper berries

½ cup red wine

salt and pepper

chopped fresh flat-leaf parsley, to garnish

Heat the oil in a large heavy pan. Add the chicken and cook, turning frequently, for 5 minutes, until golden on all sides. Using a slotted spoon, transfer to a plate lined with paper towels.

Add the onion to the pan and cook over medium heat, stirring occasionally, until softened. Stir in the cabbage and apples and cook, stirring occasionally, for 5 minutes. Add the chestnuts (if using), juniper berries, and wine and season to taste with salt and pepper. Bring to a boil.

Spoon half the cabbage mixture into the slow cooker, add the chicken pieces, then top with the remaining cabbage mixture. Cover and cook on low for 5 hours, until the chicken is tender and cooked through. Garnish with parsley and serve immediately.

Chicken in White Wine Sauce

serves 4–6

2 tbsp all-purpose flour

1 chicken, weighing
3 lb 8 oz/1.6 kg, cut into
8 pieces

4 tbsp butter

1 tbsp sunflower oil

4 shallots, finely chopped

12 white mushrooms,
sliced

2 tbsp brandy

2¼ cups dry white wine

generous 1 cup heavy
cream

salt and pepper

cooked green vegetables,
to serve

Put the flour into a plastic food bag and season to taste with salt and pepper. Add the chicken pieces, in batches, hold the top securely, and shake well to coat. Transfer the chicken to a plate.

Heat half the butter with the oil in a heavy skillet. Add the chicken pieces and cook over medium–high heat, turning frequently, for 10 minutes, until golden all over. Using a slotted spoon, transfer them to a plate.

Wipe out the skillet with paper towels, then return to medium–high heat and melt the remaining butter. Add the shallots and mushrooms and cook, stirring constantly, for 3 minutes, until the shallots are golden and the mushrooms are lightly browned. Return the chicken to the skillet and remove from the heat. Warm the brandy in a small ladle, ignite, and pour it over the chicken, shaking the skillet gently until the flames have died down.

Return the skillet to the heat and pour in the wine. Bring to a boil over low heat, scraping up any sediment from the bottom of the skillet. Transfer to the slow cooker, cover, and cook on low for 5–6 hours, until the chicken is tender and cooked through.

Transfer the chicken to a serving dish and keep warm. Skim off any fat from the surface of the cooking liquid and pour the liquid into a pan. Stir in the cream and bring just to a boil over low heat. Season to taste with salt and pepper and pour the sauce over the chicken. Serve immediately with green vegetables.

Chicken with New Potatoes & Bacon

serves 6

1 chicken, weighing
4 lb/1.8 kg

4 tbsp butter

2 tbsp olive oil

1 lb 7 oz/650 g small white
onions, peeled

1 lb 7 oz/650 g small new
potatoes

6 slices bacon, chopped

2¼ cups dry white wine

1 bouquet garni

2¼ cups hot chicken stock

salt and pepper

chopped fresh flat-leaf
parsley, to garnish

Season the chicken inside and out with salt and pepper. Melt half the butter with the oil in a large skillet. Add the chicken and cook over medium heat, turning frequently, for 8–10 minutes, until evenly browned. Remove from the pan and put it into the slow cooker, breast-side down.

Add the onions, potatoes, and bacon to the skillet and cook, stirring frequently, for 10 minutes, until lightly browned. Pour in the wine, season to taste with salt and pepper, and add the bouquet garni. Bring to a boil, then transfer the mixture to the slow cooker. Pour in the hot stock. Cover and cook, turning the chicken once halfway through cooking, for 5–6 hours, until the chicken is tender and cooked through.

Using a slotted spoon, transfer the vegetables and bacon to a bowl. Carefully remove the chicken and put it on a warmed serving dish. Arrange the vegetables around the chicken and keep warm. Remove and discard the bouquet garni.

Measure 2½ cups of the cooking liquid, pour it into a pan, and bring to a boil. Boil until slightly reduced, then whisk in the remaining butter, a little at a time. Pour the sauce into a sauceboat. Carve the chicken and transfer to individual plates with the bacon and vegetables. Garnish with parsley and serve immediately with the sauce.

Duck & Red Wine Stew

serves 4

4 duck portions, about 6 oz/175 g each

1 red onion, chopped

2–3 garlic cloves, chopped

1 large carrot, chopped

2 celery stalks, chopped

2 tbsp all-purpose flour

1¼ cups red wine

2 tbsp brandy

¾ cup chicken stock or water

3-inch/7.5-cm strip thinly pared orange rind

2 tbsp red currant jelly

1½ cups sugar snap peas

1–2 tsp olive oil

4 oz/115 g button mushrooms

salt and pepper

chopped fresh flat-leaf parsley, to garnish

Heat a heavy skillet for 1 minute, then add the duck portions, and cook over low heat until the fat runs. Increase the heat to medium and cook, turning once, for 5 minutes, until browned on both sides. Using a slotted spoon, transfer to the slow cooker.

Add the onion, garlic, carrot, and celery to the skillet and cook, stirring occasionally, for 5 minutes, until softened. Sprinkle in the flour and cook, stirring constantly, for 2 minutes, then remove the skillet from the heat. Gradually stir in the wine, brandy, and stock, return the skillet to the heat, and bring to a boil, stirring constantly. Season to taste with salt and pepper and stir in the orange rind and red currant jelly. Pour the mixture over the duck portions, cover, and cook on low, occasionally skimming off the fat from the stew, for 8 hours.

Cook the sugar snap peas in a pan of boiling water for 3 minutes, then drain. Heat the oil in a separate pan, add the mushrooms, and cook, stirring frequently, for 3 minutes. Add the sugar snap peas and mushrooms to the stew, re-cover, and cook on high for 25–30 minutes, until tender. Garnish with parsley and serve immediately.

Salmon with Spinach

serves 4

⅔ cup fish stock

1 cup dry white wine

2 lemons

1 onion, thinly sliced

4 salmon fillets, about
6 oz/175 g each

1 bouquet garni

3 lb/1.3 kg spinach, coarse
stalks removed

freshly grated nutmeg,
to taste

¾ cup unsalted butter,
plus extra for greasing

salt and pepper

Lightly grease the slow cooker pot with butter. Pour the stock and wine into a pan and bring to a boil. Meanwhile, thinly slice 1 of the lemons. Put half the lemon slices and all the onion slices over the bottom of the slow cooker pot and top with the salmon fillets. Season to taste with salt and pepper, add the bouquet garni, and cover the fish with the remaining lemon slices. Pour the hot stock mixture over the fish, cover, and cook on low for 1½ hours, until the fish flakes easily.

Meanwhile, grate the rind and squeeze the juice from the remaining lemon. When the fish is nearly ready, cook the spinach, in just the water clinging to the leaves after washing, for 3–5 minutes, until wilted. Drain well, squeezing out as much water as possible. Chop finely, arrange on warmed individual plates, and season to taste with salt, pepper, and nutmeg.

Carefully lift the fish out of the slow cooker and discard the lemon slices, onion slices, and bouquet garni. Put the salmon fillets on top of the spinach and keep warm.

Melt the butter in a pan over low heat. Stir in the lemon rind and half the juice. Taste and adjust the seasoning, adding more lemon juice, salt, and pepper if needed. Pour the lemon butter sauce over the fish and serve immediately.

Seafood Stew

serves 4

2 tbsp olive oil, plus extra for drizzling

1 large onion, chopped

4 garlic cloves, finely chopped

1 yellow bell pepper, seeded and chopped

1 red bell pepper, seeded and chopped

1 orange bell pepper, seeded and chopped

1 lb/450 g tomatoes, peeled and chopped

2 large green chiles, such as poblano, chopped

finely grated rind and juice of 1 lime

2 tbsp chopped fresh cilantro, plus extra leaves to garnish

1 bay leaf

2 cups fish, vegetable, or chicken stock

1 lb/450 g red snapper

1 lb/450 g shrimp

8 oz/225 g cleaned squid

salt and pepper

Heat the oil in a pan. Add the onion and garlic and cook over low heat, stirring occasionally, for 5 minutes, until softened. Add the bell peppers, tomatoes, and chiles and cook, stirring frequently, for 5 minutes. Stir in the lime rind and juice, add the chopped cilantro and bay leaf, and pour in the stock. Bring to a boil, stirring occasionally.

Transfer the mixture to the slow cooker, cover, and cook on low for 7½ hours. Meanwhile, skin the fish fillets, if necessary, and cut the flesh into chunks. Peel and devein the shrimp. Cut the squid bodies into rings and halve the tentacles or leave them whole.

Add the seafood to the stew, season to taste with salt and pepper, re-cover, and cook on high for 30 minutes, or until tender and cooked through. Remove and discard the bay leaf. Garnish the stew with cilantro leaves and serve immediately.

Carrot & Coriander Soup

serves 6

1 tbsp butter

1½ tbsp sunflower oil

1 Bermuda onion, finely chopped

3½ cups diced carrots

½-inch/1-cm piece fresh ginger

2 tsp ground coriander

1 tsp all-purpose flour

5 cups vegetable stock

⅔ cup sour cream

2 tbsp chopped fresh cilantro

salt and pepper

croutons, to serve

Melt the butter with the oil in a pan. Add the onion, carrots, and ginger, cover, and cook over low heat, stirring occasionally, for 8 minutes, until softened and just beginning to color.

Sprinkle over the ground coriander and flour and cook, stirring constantly, for 1 minute. Gradually stir in the stock, a little at a time, and bring to a boil, stirring constantly. Season to taste with salt and pepper.

Transfer the mixture to the slow cooker, cover, and cook on low for 4–5 hours. Ladle the soup into a food processor or blender, in batches if necessary, and process until smooth. Return the soup to the slow cooker and stir in the sour cream. Cover and cook on low for an additional 15–20 minutes, until heated through.

Ladle the soup into warmed soup bowls, sprinkle with the chopped cilantro, and top with croutons. Serve immediately.

Risotto with Spring Vegetables

serves 4

5 cups vegetable stock

large pinch of saffron threads

4 tbsp butter

1 tbsp olive oil

1 onion, chopped

2 garlic cloves, finely chopped

generous 1 cup risotto rice

3 tbsp dry white wine

1 bay leaf

9 oz/250 g mixed spring vegetables, such as asparagus spears, green beans, baby carrots, baby fava beans, and young green peas, thawed if frozen

2 tbsp chopped fresh flat-leaf parsley

2/3 cup grated Parmesan cheese

salt and pepper

Put a generous 1/3 cup of the stock into a small bowl, crumble in the saffron threads, and let steep. Reserve 2/3 cup of the remaining stock and heat the remainder in a pan.

Meanwhile, melt 2 tablespoons of the butter with the oil in a separate large pan. Add the onion and garlic and cook over low heat, stirring occasionally, for 5 minutes, until softened. Stir in the rice and cook, stirring constantly, for 1–2 minutes, until all the grains are coated and glistening. Pour in the wine and cook, stirring constantly, for a few minutes, until all the alcohol has evaporated. Season to taste with salt and pepper. Pour in the hot stock and the saffron mixture, add the bay leaf, and bring to a boil, stirring constantly.

Transfer the mixture to the slow cooker, cover, and cook on low for 2 hours. Meanwhile, if using fresh vegetables, slice the asparagus spears, green beans, and carrots and blanch all the vegetables in boiling water for 5 minutes. Drain and reserve.

Stir the reserved stock into the rice mixture, if it seems dry, and add the mixed vegetables, sprinkling them evenly over the top. Re-cover and cook on low for an additional 30–45 minutes, until heated through.

Remove and discard the bay leaf. Gently stir in the parsley, the remaining butter, and the Parmesan and serve immediately.

Vegetable Stew with Parsley Dumplings

serves 6

½ rutabaga, cut into chunks

2 onions, sliced

2 potatoes, cut into chunks

2 carrots, cut into chunks

2 celery stalks, sliced

2 zucchini, sliced

2 tbsp tomato paste

2½ cups hot vegetable stock

1 bay leaf

1 tsp ground coriander

½ tsp dried thyme

14 oz/400 g canned corn kernels, drained

salt and pepper

parsley dumplings

1¾ cups self-rising flour

pinch of salt

⅔ cup vegetable shortening

2 tbsp chopped fresh flat-leaf parsley, plus extra sprigs to garnish

about ½ cup milk

Put the rutabaga, onions, potatoes, carrots, celery, and zucchini into the slow cooker. Stir the tomato paste into the stock and pour it over the vegetables. Add the bay leaf, coriander, and thyme and season to taste with salt and pepper. Cover and cook on low for 6 hours.

To make the dumplings, sift the flour with the salt into a bowl and mix in the shortening and chopped parsley. Add just enough of the milk to make a firm but light dough. Knead lightly and shape into 12 small balls.

Stir the corn into the mixture in the slow cooker and place the dumplings on top. Cook on high for 30 minutes. Garnish with parsley sprigs and serve immediately.

Around the World

Caribbean Beef Stew

serves 6

1 lb/450 g braising beef

3½ cups diced pumpkin or other squash

1 onion, chopped

1 red bell pepper, seeded and chopped

2 garlic cloves, finely chopped

1-inch/2.5-cm piece fresh ginger, finely chopped

1 tbsp sweet or hot paprika

1 cup beef stock

14 oz/400 g canned chopped tomatoes

14 oz/400 g canned pigeon peas or chickpeas, drained and rinsed

14 oz/400 g canned black-eyed peas, drained and rinsed

salt and pepper

Trim off any visible fat from the beef, then dice the meat. Heat a large heavy pan without adding any extra fat. Add the meat and cook, stirring constantly, for a few minutes, until evenly browned. Stir in the pumpkin, onion, and bell pepper and cook for 1 minute, then add the garlic, ginger, and paprika. Pour in the stock, add the tomatoes, and bring to a boil.

Transfer the mixture to the slow cooker, cover, and cook on low for 7 hours. Add the pigeon peas and black-eyed peas to the stew and season to taste with salt and pepper. Re-cover and cook on high for 30 minutes. Serve immediately.

Neapolitan Beef

serves 6

1¼ cups red wine

4 tbsp olive oil

1 celery stalk, chopped

2 shallots, sliced

4 garlic cloves, finely chopped

1 bay leaf

10 fresh basil leaves, plus extra to garnish

3 fresh parsley sprigs

pinch of grated nutmeg

pinch of ground cinnamon

2 cloves

3 lb 5 oz/1.5 kg beef pot roast

1–2 garlic cloves, thinly sliced

2 slices bacon, chopped

14 oz/400 g canned chopped tomatoes

2 tbsp tomato paste

Combine the wine, half the oil, the celery, shallots, garlic, herbs, and spices in a large nonmetallic bowl. Add the beef, cover, and let marinate, turning occasionally, for 12 hours.

Drain the beef, reserving the marinade, and pat dry with paper towels. Make small incisions all over the beef using a sharp knife. Insert a slice of garlic and a piece of bacon in each "pocket." Heat the remaining oil in a large skillet. Add the meat and cook over medium heat, turning frequently, until evenly browned. Transfer the beef to the slow cooker.

Strain the reserved marinade into the skillet and bring to a boil. Stir in the tomatoes and tomato paste. Stir well, then pour the mixture over the beef. Cover and cook on low for about 8–9 hours, until the beef is cooked to your liking. If possible, turn the beef over halfway through the cooking time and re-cover the slow cooker immediately.

Remove the beef from the slow cooker and place on a carving board. Cover with foil and let stand for 10–15 minutes to firm up. Cut into slices and transfer to a platter. Spoon the sauce over it, garnish with basil leaves, and serve immediately.

Goulash

serves 4

4 tbsp sunflower oil

1 lb 7 oz/650 g braising beef, cut into 1-inch/2.5-cm cubes

2 tsp all-purpose flour

2 tsp paprika

1½ cups beef stock

3 onions, chopped

4 carrots, diced

1 large potato or 2 medium potatoes, diced

1 bay leaf

½–1 tsp caraway seeds

14 oz/400 g canned chopped tomatoes

2 tbsp sour cream

salt and pepper

Heat half the oil in a heavy skillet. Add the beef and cook over medium heat, stirring frequently, until evenly browned. Reduce the heat and stir in the flour and paprika. Cook, stirring constantly, for 2 minutes. Gradually stir in the stock and bring to a boil, then transfer the mixture to the slow cooker.

Wipe out the skillet with paper towels, then heat the remaining oil. Add the onions and cook over low heat, stirring occasionally, for 5 minutes, until softened. Stir in the carrots and potato and cook for an additional few minutes. Add the bay leaf, caraway seeds, and tomatoes. Season to taste with salt and pepper.

Transfer the vegetable mixture to the slow cooker and stir well, then cover and cook on low for 9 hours, until the meat is tender.

Remove and discard the bay leaf. Stir in the sour cream and serve immediately.

Jalapeño Pork Chops

serves 4

4 pork chops, trimmed of excess fat

2 tbsp corn oil

1 lb/450 g canned pineapple chunks in juice

1 red bell pepper, seeded and finely chopped

2 fresh jalapeño chiles, seeded and finely chopped

1 onion, finely chopped

1 tbsp chopped fresh cilantro, plus extra sprigs to garnish

½ cup hot chicken stock

salt and pepper

flour tortillas, to serve

Season the chops with salt and pepper to taste. Heat the oil in a large heavy skillet. Add the chops and cook over medium heat for 2–3 minutes each side, until lightly browned. Transfer them to the slow cooker. Drain the pineapple, reserving the juice, and set aside.

Add the bell pepper, chiles, and onion to the skillet and cook, stirring occasionally, for 5 minutes, until the onion has softened. Transfer the mixture to the slow cooker and add the chopped cilantro, stock, and ½ cup of the reserved pineapple juice. Cover and cook on low for 6 hours, until the chops are tender.

Add the reserved pineapple to the slow cooker, re-cover, and cook on high for 15 minutes. Garnish with cilantro sprigs and serve immediately with flour tortillas.

Spicy Indian Pork

serves 6

1 tsp cumin seeds

½–1 tsp black mustard seeds

1 tsp fenugreek seeds

1 tsp black peppercorns

4–6 dried red chiles

6 tbsp white wine vinegar

2 lb 4 oz/1 kg diced pork

1⅔ cups peeled and chopped tomatoes

1 onion, sliced

2 garlic cloves, finely chopped

1 green bell pepper, seeded and chopped

1 tbsp peanut oil

1 tsp ground cinnamon

½ tsp ground turmeric

juice and grated rind of 1 lime

1-inch/2.5-cm piece fresh ginger, finely chopped

2¼ cups water

4 tbsp chopped fresh cilantro

salt and pepper

cooked rice, to serve

Put the cumin, mustard, and fenugreek seeds, peppercorns, and dried chiles into a spice grinder or mortar and grind to a powder. Transfer to a large nonmetallic bowl and stir in the vinegar and ½ teaspoon of salt. Add the pork, tomatoes, onion, garlic, bell pepper, oil, cinnamon, turmeric, lime juice and rind, and ginger and mix well. Cover with plastic wrap and let marinate overnight in the refrigerator.

Transfer the mixture to a large pan, pour in the water, and bring to a boil, stirring frequently. Transfer to the slow cooker, cover, and cook on low for 8–9 hours, until the meat is tender.

Taste and adjust the seasoning, adding salt and pepper if needed. Stir in the chopped cilantro and serve immediately with rice.

Moroccan Lamb

serves 6

3 tbsp olive oil

2 red onions, chopped

2 garlic cloves, finely chopped

1-inch/2.5-cm piece fresh ginger, finely chopped

1 yellow bell pepper, seeded and chopped

2 lb 4 oz/1 kg boneless shoulder of lamb, trimmed and cut into 1-inch/2.5-cm cubes

3¾ cups lamb or chicken stock

1 cup plumped dried apricots, halved

1 tbsp honey

4 tbsp lemon juice

pinch of saffron threads

2-inch/5-cm cinnamon stick

salt and pepper

toasted silvered almonds and fresh cilantro sprigs, to garnish

Heat the oil in a large heavy pan. Add the onions, garlic, ginger, and bell pepper and cook over low heat, stirring occasionally, for 5 minutes, until the onion has softened. Add the lamb and stir well to mix, then pour in the stock. Add the apricots, honey, lemon juice, saffron, and cinnamon stick and season to taste with salt and pepper. Bring to a boil.

Transfer the mixture to the slow cooker. Cover and cook on low for 8½ hours, until the meat is tender.

Remove and discard the cinnamon stick. Transfer to warmed bowls and garnish with slivered almonds and cilantro sprigs. Serve immediately.

French Lamb Stew

serves 6

1¼ cups dry white wine

3 tbsp brandy

1 tbsp olive oil

1 fresh rosemary sprig

1 bay leaf

1 tbsp chopped fresh parsley

2 cloves

6 allspice berries

6 black peppercorns

1 strip thinly pared orange rind

4 shallots, sliced

2 carrots, sliced

2 garlic cloves, finely chopped

3 lb/1.3 kg diced lamb

1 cup all-purpose flour

4 slices bacon, cut into 1-inch/2.5-cm strips

2 onions, chopped

2¼ cups beef stock

salt and pepper

crusty bread, to serve

Put the wine, brandy, oil, rosemary sprig, bay leaf, parsley, cloves, allspice berries, peppercorns, orange rind, shallots, carrots, garlic, and lamb into a large nonmetallic bowl and mix well. Cover with plastic wrap and let marinate overnight in the refrigerator.

Drain the lamb cubes, reserving the marinade. Pat the lamb dry with paper towels. Put the flour into a plastic food bag and season to taste with salt and pepper. Add the lamb cubes, in batches, hold the top securely, and shake well to coat. Transfer the meat to a plate.

Cook the bacon in a large nonstick or heavy pan over medium heat for 3 minutes. Add the onions, reduce the heat, and cook, stirring occasionally, for 5 minutes, until softened. Add the lamb, increase the heat to medium, and cook, stirring frequently, for 8–10 minutes, until evenly browned. Pour in the reserved marinade and the stock and bring to a boil, stirring occasionally.

Transfer the mixture to the slow cooker, cover, and cook on low for 8–9 hours, until the meat is tender. Skim off any fat from the surface and remove and discard the rosemary sprig, bay leaf, and orange rind. Taste and adjust the seasoning, adding salt and pepper if needed. Serve immediately with crusty bread.

Sweet & Sour Chicken Wings

serves 4–6

2 lb 4 oz/1 kg chicken wings, tips removed

2 celery stalks, chopped

3 cups hot chicken stock

2 tbsp cornstarch

3 tbsp white wine vinegar or rice vinegar

3 tbsp dark soy sauce

5 tbsp sweet chili sauce

¼ cup light brown sugar

14 oz/400 g canned pineapple chunks in juice, drained

7 oz/200 g canned sliced bamboo shoots, drained and rinsed

½ green bell pepper, seeded and thinly sliced

½ red bell pepper, seeded and thinly sliced

salt

steamed bok choy, to serve

Put the chicken wings and celery in the slow cooker and season well with salt. Pour in the stock, cover, and cook on low for 5 hours.

Drain the chicken wings, reserving 1½ cups of the stock, and keep warm. Pour the reserved stock into a pan and stir in the cornstarch. Add the vinegar, soy sauce, and chili sauce. Place over medium heat and stir in the sugar. Cook, stirring constantly, for 5 minutes, or until the sugar has dissolved completely and the sauce is thickened, smooth, and clear.

Reduce the heat, stir in the pineapple, bamboo shoots, and bell peppers and simmer gently for 2–3 minutes. Stir in the chicken wings until they are thoroughly coated, then transfer to warmed bowls. Serve immediately with bok choy.

Chipotle Chicken

serves 4

4–6 dried chipotle chiles

4 garlic cloves, unpeeled

1 small onion, chopped

14 oz/400 g canned chopped tomatoes

1¼ cups hot chicken or vegetable stock

4 skinless chicken breasts

salt and pepper

chopped fresh cilantro, to garnish

Preheat the oven to 400°F/200°C. Place the chiles in a bowl and pour in just enough hot water to cover. Set aside to soak for 30 minutes. Meanwhile, place the garlic cloves on a baking sheet and roast in the preheated oven for about 10 minutes, until soft. Remove from the oven and let cool.

Drain the chiles, reserving ½ cup of the soaking water. Seed the chiles, if you like, and chop coarsely. Place the chiles and reserved soaking water in a blender or food processor and process to a paste. Peel and mash the garlic in a bowl.

Place the chile paste, garlic, onion, and tomatoes in the slow cooker and stir in the stock. Season the chicken with salt and pepper to taste and place in the slow cooker. Cover and cook on low for about 5 hours, until the chicken is tender and cooked through.

Lift the chicken out of the slow cooker with a slotted spoon, cover, and keep warm. Pour the cooking liquid into a pan and bring to a boil on the stove. Boil for 5–10 minutes, until reduced. Place the chicken on warmed plates and spoon over the sauce. Garnish with cilantro and serve immediately.

Bulgarian Chicken

serves 6

2 tbsp sunflower oil

6 chicken portions

2 onions, chopped

2 garlic cloves, finely chopped

1 fresh red chile, seeded and finely chopped

6 tomatoes, peeled and chopped

2 tsp sweet paprika

1 bay leaf

1 cup hot chicken stock

salt and pepper

Heat the oil in a large heavy skillet. Add the chicken and cook over medium heat, turning occasionally, for about 10 minutes, until evenly browned.

Transfer the chicken to the slow cooker and add the onions, garlic, chile, and tomatoes. Sprinkle in the paprika, add the bay leaf, and pour in the stock. Season to taste with salt and pepper. Stir well, cover, and cook on low for 6 hours, until the chicken is cooked through and tender. Remove and discard the bay leaf. Serve immediately.

Jambalaya

serves 6

½ tsp cayenne pepper

2 tsp chopped fresh thyme

12 oz/350 g skinless, boneless chicken breasts, diced

2 tbsp corn oil

2 onions, chopped

2 garlic cloves, finely chopped

2 green bell peppers, seeded and chopped

2 celery stalks, chopped

⅔ cup chopped smoked ham

generous 1 cup sliced chorizo sausage

14 oz/400 g canned chopped tomatoes

2 tbsp tomato paste

1 cup chicken stock

1 lb/450 g shrimp, peeled and deveined

2⅔ cups cooked rice

salt and pepper

snipped fresh chives, to garnish

Combine the cayenne pepper, ½ teaspoon of pepper, 1 teaspoon of salt, and the thyme in a bowl. Add the chicken and toss to coat.

Heat the oil in a large heavy pan. Add the onions, garlic, bell peppers, and celery and cook over low heat, stirring occasionally, for 5 minutes. Add the chicken and cook over medium heat, stirring frequently, for an additional 5 minutes, until golden all over. Stir in the ham, chorizo, tomatoes, tomato paste, and stock and bring to a boil.

Transfer the mixture to the slow cooker. Cover and cook on low for 6 hours. Add the shrimp and rice, re-cover, and cook on high for 30 minutes.

Taste and adjust the seasoning, adding salt and pepper if needed. Transfer to warmed plates, garnish with chives, and serve immediately.

Moroccan Sea Bass

serves 2

2 tbsp olive oil

2 onions, chopped

2 garlic cloves, finely chopped

2 carrots, finely chopped

1 fennel bulb, finely chopped

½ tsp ground cumin

½ tsp ground cloves

1 tsp ground coriander

pinch of saffron threads

1¼ cups fish stock

1 preserved or fresh lemon

1 whole sea bass, weighing 2 lb/900 g, cleaned

salt and pepper

Heat the oil in a large heavy pan. Add the onions, garlic, carrots, and fennel and cook over medium heat, stirring occasionally, for 5 minutes. Stir in all the spices and cook, stirring, for an additional 2 minutes. Pour in the stock, season to taste with salt and pepper, and bring to a boil.

Transfer the mixture to the slow cooker. Cover and cook on low for 6 hours, or until the vegetables are tender.

Rinse the preserved lemon, if using. Discard the fish head, if you like. Slice the lemon and place the slices in the fish cavity, then place the fish in the slow cooker. Re-cover and cook on high for 30–45 minutes, until the flesh flakes easily.

Carefully transfer the fish to a platter and spoon the vegetables around it. Cover and keep warm. Transfer the cooking liquid to a pan and boil for a few minutes, until reduced. Spoon it over the fish and serve immediately.

Salmon Chowder

serves 6

1 tbsp butter

1 tbsp sunflower oil

1 onion, finely chopped

1 leek, finely chopped

1 fennel bulb, finely chopped, feathery tops reserved

2 potatoes, diced

generous 3 cups fish stock

1 lb/450 g salmon fillet, skinned and cut into cubes

1¼ cups milk

1⅔ cups light cream

2 tbsp chopped fresh dill

salt and pepper

Melt the butter with the oil in a pan. Add the onion, leek, and fennel and cook over low heat, stirring occasionally, for 5 minutes. Add the potatoes and cook, stirring occasionally, for an additional 4 minutes, then pour in the stock and season to taste with salt and pepper. Bring to a boil, then transfer to the slow cooker. Cover and cook on low for 3 hours, until the potatoes are tender.

Meanwhile, chop the fennel fronds and set aside. Add the salmon to the slow cooker, pour in the milk, and stir gently. Re-cover and cook on low for 30 minutes, until the fish flakes easily.

Gently stir in the cream, dill, and the reserved fennel fronds, re-cover, and cook for an additional 10–15 minutes, until heated through. Taste and adjust the seasoning, adding salt and pepper if needed. Serve immediately.

Vegetarian Paella

serves 6

4 tbsp olive oil

1 Bermuda onion, sliced

2 garlic cloves, finely chopped

4 cups hot vegetable stock

large pinch of saffron threads, lightly crushed

1 yellow bell pepper, seeded and sliced

1 red bell pepper, seeded and sliced

1 large eggplant, diced

1⅓ cups paella or risotto rice

1½ cups peeled and chopped tomatoes

1⅔ cups sliced cremini mushrooms

1 cup halved green beans

14 oz/400 g canned borlotti beans, drained and rinsed

salt and pepper

Heat the oil in a large skillet. Add the onion and garlic and cook over low heat, stirring occasionally, for 5 minutes, until softened. Meanwhile, put 3 tablespoons of the hot stock into a small bowl and stir in the saffron, then let steep.

Add the bell peppers and eggplant to the skillet and cook, stirring occasionally, for 5 minutes. Add the rice and cook, stirring constantly, for 1 minute, until the grains are coated with oil and glistening. Pour in the remaining stock and add the tomatoes, mushrooms, green beans, and borlotti beans. Stir in the saffron mixture and season to taste with salt and pepper.

Transfer the mixture to the slow cooker, cover, and cook on low for 2½–3 hours, until the rice is tender and stock has been absorbed. Serve immediately.

Vegetable Curry

serves 4–6

2 tbsp vegetable oil

1 tsp cumin seeds

1 onion, sliced

2 curry leaves

1-inch/2.5-cm piece fresh ginger, finely chopped

2 fresh red chiles, seeded and chopped

2 tbsp Indian curry paste

2 carrots, sliced

1½ cups snow peas

1 head of cauliflower, cut into florets

3 tomatoes, peeled and chopped

¾ cup frozen peas, thawed

½ tsp ground turmeric

⅔–1 cup hot vegetable or chicken stock

salt and pepper

naan, to serve

Heat the oil in a large heavy pan. Add the cumin seeds and cook, stirring constantly, for 1–2 minutes, until they give off their aroma and begin to pop. Add the onion and curry leaves and cook, stirring occasionally, for 5 minutes, until the onion has softened. Add the ginger and chiles and cook, stirring occasionally, for 1 minute.

Stir in the curry paste and cook, stirring, for 2 minutes, then add the carrots, snow peas, and cauliflower. Cook for 5 minutes, then add the tomatoes, peas, and turmeric and season to taste with salt and pepper. Cook for 3 minutes, then add ⅔ cup of the stock and bring to a boil.

Transfer the mixture to the slow cooker. If the vegetables are not covered, add more hot stock, then cover and cook on low for 5 hours, until tender. Remove and discard the curry leaves. Serve immediately with naan.

4

Entertaining

Beef Bourguignon

serves 6

2 tbsp all-purpose flour

2 lb/900 g braising beef, trimmed and cut into 1-inch/2.5-cm cubes

6 slices bacon, chopped

3 tbsp olive oil

2 tbsp unsalted butter

12 pearl onions or shallots

2 garlic cloves, finely chopped

⅔ cup beef stock

2 cups full-bodied red wine

1 bouquet garni

2 cups sliced mushrooms

salt and pepper

Put the flour into a plastic food bag and season to taste with salt and pepper. Add the beef cubes, in batches, hold the top securely, and shake well to coat. Transfer the meat to a plate.

Cook the bacon in a large heavy pan, stirring occasionally, until the fat runs and the bacon is crisp. Using a slotted spoon, transfer the bacon to a plate. Add the oil to the pan. When it is hot, add the beef cubes and cook, in batches, stirring occasionally, for 5 minutes, until evenly browned. Transfer to the plate with a slotted spoon.

Add the butter to the pan. When it has melted, add the onions and garlic and cook, stirring occasionally, for 5 minutes. Return the bacon and beef to the pan and pour in the stock and wine. Bring to a boil.

Transfer the mixture to the slow cooker and add the bouquet garni. Cover and cook on low for 7 hours, until the meat is tender.

Add the mushrooms to the slow cooker and stir well. Re-cover and cook on high for 15 minutes.

Remove and discard the bouquet garni. Taste and adjust the seasoning, adding salt and pepper if needed. Serve immediately.

Rich Beef & Coffee Stew

serves 6

4 tbsp sunflower oil

3 lb/1.3 kg braising beef, cut into 1-inch/2.5-cm cubes

4 onions, sliced

1 garlic clove, finely chopped

5 tbsp all-purpose flour

1¼ cups red wine

pinch of dried oregano

1 small fresh rosemary sprig

2¼ cups black coffee

salt and pepper

fresh marjoram sprigs, to garnish

mashed sweet potatoes, to serve

Heat the oil in a large skillet. Add the beef and cook over medium heat, stirring frequently, for 8–10 minutes, until evenly browned. Transfer to the slow cooker with a slotted spoon.

Add the onions and garlic to the skillet, reduce the heat, and cook, stirring occasionally, for 10 minutes, until softened and just beginning to color. Stir in the flour and cook, stirring constantly, for 1 minute. Gradually stir in the wine, a little at a time. Add the oregano and rosemary sprig and season to taste with salt and pepper. Pour in the coffee and bring to a boil, stirring constantly.

Transfer the mixture to the slow cooker. Cover and cook on low for 8–9 hours, until the meat is tender. Remove and discard the rosemary sprig. Taste and adjust the seasoning, adding salt and pepper if needed. Garnish with marjoram sprigs and serve immediately with mashed sweet potatoes.

Chinese Beef

serves 6

4 dried Chinese tree ear mushrooms

4 tbsp peanut oil

2 lb 4 oz/1 kg top round steak, cut into 1-inch/2.5-cm cubes

3 tbsp dark soy sauce

2 tbsp Chinese rice wine or dry sherry

1 tbsp tomato paste

1-inch/2.5-cm piece fresh ginger, very finely chopped

2 garlic cloves, very finely chopped

2 tbsp light brown sugar

1 tsp Chinese five-spice powder

3 cups beef stock

5 carrots, thinly sliced diagonally

cooked egg noodles, to serve

Put the mushrooms into a heatproof bowl and pour in warm water to cover. Set aside to soak for 20 minutes.

Meanwhile, heat the oil in a large pan. Add the beef, in batches, and cook over medium heat, stirring frequently, for 8–10 minutes, until evenly browned. Remove with a slotted spoon and drain on paper towels.

Drain the mushrooms, discarding the soaking water, and gently squeeze out any excess liquid. Cut off and discard the stems, slice the caps, and put them into a bowl. Add the soy sauce, rice wine, tomato paste, ginger, garlic, sugar, five-spice powder, and stock and mix well.

When all the meat has been browned, wipe out the pan with paper towels. Return the meat to the pan, stir in the mushroom mixture, and bring to a boil.

Transfer the mixture to the slow cooker, cover, and cook on low for 8 hours, until the meat is tender. Stir in the carrots, re-cover, and cook on high for an additional 45–60 minutes, until the carrots are tender. Serve immediately with noodles.

Pork with Almonds

serves 4

2 tbsp corn or sunflower oil

2 onions, chopped

2 garlic cloves, finely chopped

2-inch/5-cm cinnamon stick

3 cloves

1 cup ground almonds

1 lb 10 oz/750 g boneless pork, cut into 1-inch/ 2.5-cm cubes

4 tomatoes, peeled and chopped

2 tbsp capers

1 cup pitted green olives

3 pickled jalapeño chiles, drained, seeded, and cut into rings

1½ cups chicken stock

salt and pepper

Heat half the oil in a large heavy skillet. Add the onions and cook over low heat, stirring occasionally, for 5 minutes, until softened. Add the garlic, cinnamon stick, cloves, and ground almonds and cook, stirring frequently, for 8–10 minutes. Be careful not to burn the almonds.

Remove and discard the cinnamon stick and cloves and transfer the mixture to a food processor. Process to a smooth paste.

Wipe out the skillet with paper towels, then return to the heat. Heat the remaining oil, then add the pork, in batches if necessary. Cook over medium heat, stirring frequently, for 5–10 minutes, until evenly browned.

Add the almond paste, tomatoes, capers, olives, chiles, and stock to the skillet. Bring to a boil, then transfer to the slow cooker. Season to taste with salt and pepper and mix well. Cover and cook on low for 5 hours. Transfer to warmed plates and serve immediately.

Pork with Bell Peppers & Apricots

serves 4

2 tbsp olive oil

4 pork chops, trimmed of excess fat

1 shallot, chopped

2 garlic cloves, finely chopped

2 orange bell peppers, seeded and sliced

1 tbsp all-purpose flour

2½ cups chicken stock

1 tbsp medium–hot Indian curry paste

½ cup plumped dried apricots

salt and pepper

baby spinach leaves and cooked couscous, to serve

Heat the oil in a large skillet. Add the chops and cook over medium heat for 2–4 minutes on each side, until evenly browned. Remove with tongs and put them into the slow cooker.

Add the shallot, garlic, and bell peppers to the skillet, reduce the heat, and cook, stirring occasionally, for 5 minutes, until softened. Stir in the flour and cook, stirring constantly, for 1 minute. Gradually stir in the stock, a little at a time, then add the curry paste and apricots. Bring to a boil, stirring occasionally.

Season to taste with salt and pepper and transfer the mixture to the slow cooker. Cover and cook on low for 8–9 hours, until the meat is tender. Serve immediately with baby spinach and couscous.

Springtime Lamb with Asparagus

serves 4

2 tbsp sunflower oil

1 onion, thinly sliced

2 garlic cloves, very finely chopped

2 lb 4 oz/1 kg boneless shoulder of lamb, cut into 1-inch/2.5-cm cubes

8 oz/225 g asparagus spears, thawed if frozen

1¼ cups chicken stock

4 tbsp lemon juice

⅔ cup heavy cream

salt and pepper

Heat the oil in a large heavy skillet. Add the onion and cook over medium heat, stirring occasionally, for 5 minutes, until softened. Add the garlic and lamb and cook, stirring occasionally, for an additional 5 minutes, until the lamb is evenly browned.

Meanwhile, trim off and set aside the tips of the asparagus spears. Cut each of the stalks into 2–3 pieces. Add the stock and lemon juice to the skillet, season to taste with salt and pepper, and bring to a boil. Reduce the heat, add the asparagus stalks, and simmer for 2 minutes.

Transfer the mixture to the slow cooker. Cover and cook on low for 7 hours, until the lamb is tender.

About 10 minutes before the end of the cooking time, cook the reserved asparagus tips in a pan of lightly salted boiling water for 5 minutes. Drain well, then combine with the cream. Spoon the cream mixture on top of the lamb mixture, but do not stir it in. Re-cover and cook on high for 15–20 minutes to heat through. Serve immediately.

Lamb Shanks with Olives

serves 4

1½ tbsp all-purpose flour

4 lamb shanks

2 tbsp olive oil

1 onion, sliced

2 garlic cloves, finely chopped

2 tsp sweet paprika

14 oz/400 g canned chopped tomatoes

2 tbsp tomato paste

2 carrots, sliced

2 tsp sugar

1 cup red wine

2-inch/5-cm cinnamon stick

2 fresh rosemary sprigs

1 cup pitted black olives

2 tbsp lemon juice

2 tbsp chopped fresh mint, plus extra leaves to garnish

salt and pepper

Put the flour into a plastic food bag and season to taste with salt and pepper. Add the lamb shanks, hold the top securely, and shake well to coat.

Heat the oil in a large heavy pan. Add the lamb shanks and cook over medium heat, turning frequently, for 6–8 minutes, until evenly browned. Transfer to a plate and set aside.

Add the onion and garlic to the pan and cook, stirring frequently, for 5 minutes, until softened. Stir in the paprika and cook for 1 minute. Add the tomatoes, tomato paste, carrots, sugar, wine, cinnamon stick, and rosemary sprigs and bring to a boil.

Transfer the mixture to the slow cooker and add the lamb shanks. Cover and cook on low for 8 hours, until the lamb is very tender.

Add the olives, lemon juice, and chopped mint to the slow cooker. Re-cover and cook on high for 30 minutes. Remove and discard the rosemary sprigs and cinnamon stick. Garnish with mint leaves and serve immediately.

Chicken Cacciatore

serves 4

3 tbsp olive oil

4 skinless chicken portions

2 onions, sliced

2 garlic cloves, finely chopped

14 oz/400 g canned chopped tomatoes

1 tbsp tomato paste

2 tbsp chopped fresh parsley

2 tsp fresh thyme leaves, plus extra sprigs to garnish

⅔ cup red wine

salt and pepper

Heat the oil in a heavy skillet. Add the chicken and cook over medium heat, turning occasionally, for 10 minutes, until golden all over. Using a slotted spoon, transfer the chicken to the slow cooker.

Add the onions to the skillet and cook, stirring occasionally, for 5 minutes, until softened and just turning golden. Add the garlic, tomatoes, tomato paste, parsley, thyme leaves, and wine. Season to taste with salt and pepper and bring to a boil.

Pour the tomato mixture over the chicken pieces. Cover and cook on low for 5 hours, until the chicken is tender and cooked through. Taste and adjust the seasoning, adding salt and pepper if needed. Garnish with thyme sprigs and serve immediately.

Nutty Chicken

serves 4

3 tbsp sunflower oil

4 skinless chicken portions

2 shallots, chopped

1 tsp ground ginger

1 tbsp all-purpose flour

scant 2 cups beef stock

½ cup walnut pieces

grated rind of 1 lemon

2 tbsp lemon juice

1 tbsp molasses

salt and pepper

pea shoots, to garnish

Heat the oil in a large heavy skillet. Season the chicken portions with salt and pepper to taste and add to the skillet. Cook over medium heat, turning occasionally, for 5–8 minutes, until lightly golden all over. Transfer to the slow cooker.

Add the shallots to the skillet and cook, stirring occasionally, for 3–4 minutes, until softened. Sprinkle in the ginger and flour and cook, stirring constantly, for 1 minute. Gradually stir in the stock and bring to a boil, stirring constantly. Reduce the heat and simmer for 1 minute, then stir in the walnuts, lemon rind and juice, and molasses.

Pour the sauce over the chicken. Cover and cook on low for 6 hours, until the chicken is cooked through and tender. Taste and adjust the seasoning, adding salt and pepper if needed. Transfer the chicken to warmed plates and spoon some of the sauce over each portion. Garnish with pea shoots and serve immediately.

Chicken Parmigiana

serves 4

4 chicken portions,
about 9 oz/250 g each

scant ½ cup olive oil

3 red onions, thinly sliced

2 garlic cloves, finely
chopped

1 red bell pepper, seeded
and thinly sliced

1⅔ cups sliced mushrooms

2 tsp chopped fresh thyme

1 tbsp chopped fresh
flat-leaf parsley

14 oz/400 g canned
chopped tomatoes

4 tbsp dry white vermouth

scant 2 cups chicken stock

1 cup grated Parmesan
cheese

salt and pepper

cooked pappardelle,
to serve

Season the chicken with salt and pepper to taste. Heat the oil in a large pan. Add the chicken and cook over medium heat for 5–6 minutes on each side, until evenly browned. Using tongs, transfer the chicken to the slow cooker.

Add the onions, garlic, bell pepper, mushrooms, thyme, parsley, tomatoes, vermouth, and stock to the pan. Season to taste with salt and pepper and bring to a boil, stirring occasionally. Transfer the mixture to the slow cooker, cover, and cook on low for 8–9 hours, until the chicken is cooked through and tender.

Taste and adjust the seasoning, adding salt and pepper if needed. Transfer to warmed plates and sprinkle over the Parmesan. Serve immediately with pappardelle.

Duckling with Apples

serves 4

4–4 lb 8 oz/1.8–2 kg
duckling, cut into
8 pieces

2 tbsp olive oil

1 onion, finely chopped

1 carrot, finely chopped

1¼ cups chicken stock

1¼ cups dry white wine

1 bouquet garni

4 apples

4 tbsp unsalted butter

salt and pepper

Season the duckling pieces with salt and pepper to taste. Heat the oil in a large heavy skillet. Add all the duckling pieces, placing the breast portions skin-side down. Cook over medium–high heat for a few minutes, until golden brown, then transfer the breast portions to a plate. Turn the other pieces and continue to cook until browned all over. Transfer to the plate.

Add the onion and carrot to the skillet and cook over low heat, stirring occasionally, for 5 minutes, until the onion has softened. Add the stock and wine and bring to a boil.

Transfer the vegetable mixture to the slow cooker. Add the duckling pieces and the bouquet garni. Cover and cook on low, occasionally skimming off the fat from the stew, for 8 hours.

Shortly before serving, peel, core, and slice the apples. Melt the butter in a large skillet. Add the apple slices and cook over medium heat, turning occasionally, for 5 minutes, until golden.

Spoon the cooked apples onto warmed plates and divide the duckling pieces among them. Skim off the fat from the cooking liquid, then spoon the liquid and vegetables over the duckling pieces and serve immediately.

Bouillabaisse

serves 6

5 lb/2.25 kg mixed white fish, such as red snapper, porgy, sea bass, monkfish, and whiting, filleted and bones and heads reserved, if possible

1 lb/450 g jumbo shrimp

grated rind of 1 orange

pinch of saffron threads

4 garlic cloves, finely chopped

1 cup olive oil

2 onions, finely chopped

1 leek, thinly sliced

4 potatoes, thinly sliced

2 large tomatoes, peeled and chopped

1 bunch fresh flat-leaf parsley, chopped

1 fresh fennel sprig

1 fresh thyme sprig

1 bay leaf

2 cloves

6 black peppercorns

1 strip thinly pared orange rind

sea salt

lightly toasted crusty bread, to serve

Cut the fish fillets into bite-size pieces. Peel and devein the shrimp, reserving the heads and shells. Rinse the fish bones, if using, and cut off the gills of any fish heads. Place the chunks of fish and the shrimp in a large bowl. Sprinkle with the grated orange rind, saffron, half the garlic, and 2 tablespoons of the oil. Cover and set aside in the refrigerator.

Put the remaining garlic, the onions, leek, potatoes, tomatoes, parsley, fennel, thyme, bay leaf, cloves, peppercorns, and strip of orange rind into the slow cooker. Add the fish heads and bones, if using, and the shrimp shells and heads. Pour in the remaining oil and enough boiling water to cover the ingredients by 1 inch/2.5 cm. Season to taste with sea salt. Cover and cook on low for 8 hours.

Strain the stock and return the liquid to the slow cooker. Discard the flavorings and the fish and shrimp trimmings but reserve the vegetables and return them to the slow cooker if you like. Add the fish and shrimp mixture, re-cover, and cook on high for 30 minutes, until the fish is cooked through and flakes easily.

Ladle into warmed bowls and serve immediately with toasted crusty bread.

Creamed Sole & Shrimp

serves 4

2 lb/900 g potatoes, cut into chunks

1 lb 9 oz/700 g sole fillets

2 tbsp butter, plus extra for greasing

2 egg yolks

1½ cups grated cheddar cheese

1 tbsp chopped fresh flat-leaf parsley, plus extra sprigs to garnish

1 lb 4 oz/550 g cooked peeled shrimp

salt and pepper

Put the potatoes into a pan with water to cover, add a pinch of salt, and bring to a boil. Reduce the heat, cover, and cook for 20–25 minutes, until soft but not falling apart.

Meanwhile, grease a 5-cup heatproof bowl with butter, then line it with the fish fillets, skin-side inward and with the tail ends overlapping the rim. Cut out a double round of wax paper that is 2 inches/5 cm wider than the rim of the bowl. Grease 1 side with butter.

Drain the potatoes in a colander. Return to the pan, add the butter, and reheat gently until it has melted. Remove from the heat and mash well, then stir in the egg yolks, cheese, and chopped parsley. Season lightly with salt and pepper.

Make alternating layers of the mashed potato mixture and shrimp in the prepared bowl, then fold over the overlapping fish fillets. Cover the bowl with the wax paper rounds and tie in place with kitchen string.

Stand the bowl on a trivet in the slow cooker and pour in enough boiling water to come about halfway up the side. Cover and cook on low for 2½ hours.

Carefully remove the bowl from the slow cooker and discard the wax paper. Turn out onto a warmed serving dish. Garnish with parsley sprigs and serve immediately.

Stuffed Cabbage with Tomato Sauce

serves 6

1 cup finely ground
mixed nuts

2 onions, finely chopped

1 garlic clove, finely
chopped

2 celery stalks, finely
chopped

1 cup grated cheddar
cheese

1 tsp finely chopped
fresh thyme

2 eggs

1 tsp yeast extract

12 large green cabbage
leaves

tomato sauce

2 tbsp sunflower oil

2 onions, chopped

2 garlic cloves, finely
chopped

1 lb 5 oz/600 g canned
chopped tomatoes

2 tbsp tomato paste

1½ tsp sugar

1 bay leaf

salt and pepper

First, make the tomato sauce. Heat the oil in a heavy pan. Add the onions and cook over medium heat, stirring occasionally, for 5 minutes, until softened. Stir in the garlic and cook for 1 minute, then add the tomatoes, tomato paste, sugar, and bay leaf. Season to taste with salt and pepper and bring to a boil. Reduce the heat and simmer gently for 20 minutes, until thickened.

Meanwhile, combine the nuts, onions, garlic, celery, cheese, and thyme in a bowl. Lightly beat the eggs with the yeast extract in a pitcher, then stir into the nut mixture. Set aside.

Cut out the thick stalk from the cabbage leaves. Blanch the leaves in a large pan of boiling water for 5 minutes, then drain and refresh under cold water. Pat dry with paper towels.

Place a little of the nut mixture on the stalk end of each cabbage leaf. Fold the sides over, then roll up to make a neat package.

Arrange the cabbage rolls in the slow cooker, seam-side down. Remove and discard the bay leaf from the tomato sauce and pour the sauce over the cabbage rolls. Cover and cook on low for 3–4 hours. Serve the cabbage rolls hot or cold.

5

Something
Sweet

Italian Bread Pudding

serves 6

unsalted butter,
for greasing

6 slices panettone

3 tbsp Marsala wine

1¼ cups milk

1¼ cups light cream

½ cup superfine sugar

grated rind of ½ lemon

pinch of ground cinnamon

3 extra large eggs,
lightly beaten

Grease a heatproof bowl. Place the panettone on a deep plate and sprinkle with the Marsala wine.

Pour the milk and cream into a pan and add the sugar, lemon rind, and cinnamon. Gradually bring to a boil over low heat, stirring until the sugar has dissolved. Remove the pan from the heat and let cool slightly, then pour the mixture onto the eggs, beating constantly.

Place the panettone in the prepared bowl, pour in the egg mixture, and cover with aluminum foil. Stand the bowl on a trivet in the slow cooker and pour in enough boiling water to come about one-third of the way up the side of the bowl. Cover and cook on high for 2½ hours, until set.

Carefully remove the bowl from the slow cooker and discard the foil. Let cool, then chill in the refrigerator until required. Run a knife around the inside of the bowl, then turn out onto a serving dish. Serve immediately.

Blushing Pears

serves 6

6 small ripe pears

1 cup ruby port

1 cup superfine sugar

1 tsp finely chopped
candied ginger

2 tbsp lemon juice

whipped cream or strained
plain yogurt, to serve

Peel the pears, cut them in half lengthwise, and scoop out the cores. Place them in the slow cooker.

Combine the port, sugar, ginger, and lemon juice in a pitcher and pour the mixture over the pears. Cover and cook on low for 4 hours, until the pears are tender.

Let the pears cool in the slow cooker, then carefully transfer to a bowl and chill in the refrigerator until required.

To serve, cut each pear half into about 6 slices lengthwise, leaving the fruit intact at the stalk end. Carefully lift the pear halves onto serving plates and press gently to fan out the slices. Spoon the cooking juices over the pears and serve immediately with cream or yogurt.

Rice Pudding

serves 4

²⁄₃ cup short-grain rice

4 cups milk

generous ½ cup sugar

1 tsp vanilla extract

ground cinnamon,
to decorate

Rinse the rice well under cold running water and drain thoroughly. Pour the milk in a large heavy pan, add the sugar, and bring to a boil, stirring constantly. Sprinkle in the rice, stir well, and simmer gently for 10–15 minutes. Transfer the mixture to a heatproof bowl and cover with aluminum foil.

Stand the bowl on a trivet in the slow cooker and pour in enough boiling water to come about one-third of the way up the side of the bowl. Cover and cook on high for 2 hours.

Carefully remove the bowl from the slow cooker and discard the foil. Stir the vanilla extract into the rice, then spoon it into warmed bowls. Lightly dust with cinnamon and serve immediately.

Thai Black Rice Pudding

serves 4

scant 1 cup black glutinous rice

2 tbsp light brown sugar

2 cups canned coconut milk

1 cup water

3 eggs

2 tbsp superfine sugar

Combine the rice, brown sugar, and half the coconut milk in a pan, then stir in the water. Bring to a boil, then reduce the heat and simmer, stirring occasionally, for 15 minutes, until almost all the liquid has been absorbed. Transfer the mixture to a heatproof bowl.

Lightly beat the eggs with the remaining coconut milk and the superfine sugar. Strain the mixture over the rice.

Cover the bowl with aluminum foil. Stand the bowl on a trivet in the slow cooker and pour in enough boiling water to come about one-third of the way up the side of the bowl. Cover and cook on high for 2–2½ hours, until set. Carefully remove the bowl from the slow cooker and discard the foil. Serve hot or cold.

Apple Crumble

serves 4

½ cup all-purpose flour

½ cup rolled oats

⅔ cup light brown sugar

½ tsp freshly grated nutmeg

½ tsp ground cinnamon

1 cup softened unsalted butter

4 baking apples, peeled, cored, and sliced

4–5 tbsp apple juice

strained plain yogurt, to serve

Sift the flour into a bowl and stir in the oats, sugar, nutmeg, and cinnamon. Add the butter and mix in with a pastry blender or the tines of a fork.

Place the apple slices in the bottom of the slow cooker and add the apple juice. Sprinkle the flour mixture evenly over them.

Cover and cook on low for 5½ hours. Serve hot, warm, or cold with yogurt.

Magic Lemon Sponge Cake

serves 4

¾ cup superfine sugar

3 eggs, separated

1¼ cups milk

3 tbsp self-rising flour, sifted

⅔ cup lemon juice

confectioners' sugar, for dusting

Using an electric mixer, beat the superfine sugar with the egg yolks in a bowl. Gradually beat in the milk, followed by the flour and lemon juice.

Whisk the egg whites in a separate grease-free bowl until stiff. Fold half the whites into the yolk mixture, using a spatula in a figure-eight movement, then fold in the remainder. Try not to knock out the air.

Pour the mixture into a heatproof bowl and cover with aluminum foil. Stand the bowl on a trivet in the slow cooker and pour in enough boiling water to come about one-third of the way up the side of the bowl. Cover and cook on high for 2½ hours, until the mixture has set and the sauce and sponge have separated.

Carefully remove the bowl from the slow cooker and discard the foil. Transfer to warmed bowls, lightly dust with confectioners' sugar, and serve immediately.

Crème Brûlée

serves 6

1 vanilla bean

4 cups heavy cream

6 egg yolks

½ cup superfine sugar

scant ½ cup light brown sugar

Using a sharp knife, split the vanilla bean in half lengthwise, scrape the seeds into a pan, and add the bean. Pour in the cream and bring just to a boil, stirring constantly. Remove from the heat, cover, and let steep for 20 minutes.

Whisk together the egg yolks and superfine sugar in a bowl until thoroughly mixed. Remove and discard the vanilla bean from the pan, then whisk the cream into the egg yolk mixture. Strain the mixture into a large pitcher.

Divide the mixture among 6 individual baking dishes and cover with aluminum foil. Stand the dishes on a trivet in the slow cooker and pour in enough boiling water to come about halfway up the sides of the dishes. Cover and cook on low for 3–3½ hours, until just set. Remove the slow cooker pot from the base unit and let cool completely, then remove the dishes and chill in the refrigerator for at least 4 hours.

Preheat the broiler. Sprinkle the brown sugar evenly over the surface of each dessert, then cook under the preheated broiler for 30–60 seconds, until the sugar has melted and caramelized. Alternatively, you can use a cook's blowtorch. Return the dishes to the refrigerator and chill for an additional hour before serving.

Chocolate Mousse

serves 6

1¼ cups light cream

1¼ cups milk

8 oz/225 g bittersweet chocolate, broken into small pieces

1 extra large egg

4 egg yolks

4 tbsp superfine sugar

⅔ cup heavy cream

chocolate curls, to decorate

Pour the light cream and milk into a pan and add the chocolate. Set the pan over very low heat and stir until the chocolate has melted and the mixture is smooth. Remove from the heat and let cool for 10 minutes.

Beat together the egg, egg yolks, and sugar in a bowl until combined. Gradually stir in the chocolate mixture until thoroughly blended. Strain into a pitcher.

Divide the mixture among 6 individual baking dishes and cover with aluminum foil. Stand the dishes on a trivet in the slow cooker and pour in enough boiling water to come about halfway up the sides of the dishes. Cover and cook on low for 3–3½ hours, until just set. Remove the slow cooker pot from the base unit and let cool completely, then remove the dishes and chill in the refrigerator for at least 4 hours.

Whip the heavy cream in a bowl until it holds soft peaks. Top each chocolate mousse with cream and decorate with chocolate curls. Serve immediately.

Sponge Cake with Toffee Sauce

serves 6

1 cup chopped toasted hazelnuts

1/2 cup unsalted butter, plus extra for greasing

generous 1/2 cup dark brown sugar

2 eggs, lightly beaten

1 cup self-rising flour

1 tbsp lemon juice

toffee sauce

4 tbsp unsalted butter

generous 1/4 cup dark brown sugar

4 tbsp heavy cream

1 tbsp lemon juice

Grease a 3³/4-cup heatproof bowl and sprinkle half the nuts over the bottom. Cut out a double circle of wax paper that is 2³/4 inches/7 cm larger than the rim of the bowl. Make a pleat in the center.

To make the toffee sauce, put the butter, sugar, cream, and lemon juice into a pan. Set the pan over very low heat and stir until the sauce is smooth and thoroughly combined. Remove the pan from the heat. Pour half the mixture into the prepared bowl and swirl gently to coat part of the side. Reserve the remainder.

Beat together the butter and sugar in a bowl until light and fluffy. Gradually beat in the eggs, then gently fold in the flour, lemon juice, and the remaining nuts. Spoon the mixture into the bowl. Cover with the double wax paper circle and tie with kitchen string.

Put the bowl into the slow cooker and pour in boiling water to come about halfway up the side. Cover and cook on high for 3–3¹/4 hours, until just set.

Shortly before serving, gently reheat the reserved toffee sauce. Carefully remove the bowl from the slow cooker and discard the wax paper. Run a knife around the inside of the bowl, then turn out onto a warmed serving dish. Pour the sauce over the sponge cake and serve immediately.

Almond Sponge Cake

serves 4

unsalted butter,
for greasing

10–12 ladyfingers

1¼ cups milk

2 eggs

2 tbsp superfine sugar

½ cup chopped blanched
almonds

4–5 drops of almond
extract

sherry sauce

1 tbsp superfine sugar

3 egg yolks

⅔ cup sweet sherry

Grease a 2½-cup heatproof bowl. Line the bowl with the ladyfingers, cutting them to fit and placing them cut-sides down and sugar-coated sides outward. Cover the bottom of the bowl with some of the trimmings.

Pour the milk into a pan and bring just to a boil, then remove from the heat. Beat together the eggs and sugar in a heatproof bowl until combined, then stir in the milk. Stir in the almonds and almond extract.

Carefully pour the mixture into the prepared bowl, making sure that the ladyfingers stay in place, and cover the bowl with aluminum foil. Stand the bowl on a trivet in the slow cooker and pour in enough boiling water to come about halfway up the side of the dish. Cover and cook on high for 3–3½ hours, until set.

Shortly before serving, make the sherry sauce. Put the sugar, egg yolks, and sherry into a heatproof bowl. Set the bowl over a pan of simmering water, without letting the bottom of the bowl touch the surface of the water. Whisk well until the mixture thickens, but do not let it boil. Remove from the heat.

Carefully remove the bowl from the slow cooker and discard the foil. Let stand for 2–3 minutes, then turn out onto a warmed serving plate. Pour the sherry sauce around it and serve immediately.

Poached Peaches in Marsala Wine

serves 4–6

2/3 cup water,
plus 2 tbsp

2/3 cup Marsala wine

4 tbsp superfine sugar

1 vanilla bean,
split lengthwise

6 peaches, cut into wedges
and pitted or 12 apricots,
halved and pitted

2 tsp cornstarch

strained plain yogurt,
to serve

Pour the 2/3 cup of water and the Marsala wine into a pan and add the sugar and vanilla bean. Set the pan over low heat and stir until the sugar has dissolved, then bring to a boil without stirring. Remove from the heat.

Put the peaches into the slow cooker and pour the syrup over them. Cover and cook on high for 1–1½ hours, until the fruit is tender.

Using a slotted spoon, gently transfer the peaches to a serving dish. Remove the vanilla bean from the slow cooker and scrape the seeds into the syrup with the point of a knife. Discard the bean. Stir the cornstarch to a paste with the 2 tablespoons of water in a small bowl, then stir into the syrup. Re-cover and cook on high for 15 minutes, stirring occasionally.

Spoon the syrup over the fruit and let cool. Serve warm or chill in the refrigerator for 2 hours before serving with yogurt.

Chocolate & Walnut Sponge Cake

serves 4–6

½ cup unsweetened cocoa, plus extra for dusting

2 tbsp milk

1 cup self-rising flour

pinch of salt

½ cup softened unsalted butter, plus extra for greasing

generous ½ cup superfine sugar

2 eggs, lightly beaten

½ cup chopped walnuts

whipped cream, to serve

Grease a 5-cup heatproof bowl. Cut out a double circle of wax paper that is 2¾-inches/7 cm wider than the rim of the bowl. Grease 1 side with butter and make a pleat in the center.

Mix the cocoa with the milk to a paste in a small bowl. Sift the flour and salt into a separate small bowl.

Beat together the butter and sugar in a large bowl until pale and fluffy. Gradually beat in the eggs, a little at a time, then gently fold in the sifted flour, followed by the cocoa mixture and the walnuts.

Spoon the mixture into the prepared bowl. Cover the bowl with the wax paper circle, buttered-side down, and tie in place with kitchen string. Stand the bowl on a trivet in the slow cooker and pour in enough boiling water to come about halfway up the side of the bowl. Cover and cook on high for 3–3½ hours.

Carefully remove the bowl from the slow cooker and discard the wax paper. Run a knife around the inside of the bowl, then turn out onto a warmed serving dish. Serve immediately with whipped cream, dusted with cocoa.